HOW TO GET RID OF YOUR BOSS

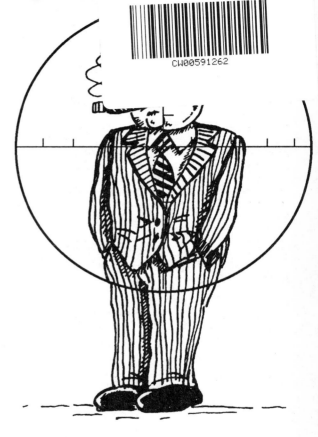

Mogul & CLYDE

Take That Books is an imprint of
Take That Ltd.
P.O.Box 200
Harrogate
HG1 2YR

ISBN 0-9519489-1-1

Layout, illustrations and typesetting by Take That Ltd., P.O.Box 200, Harrogate, HG1 2YR.

Printed and bound in Great Britain.

TAKE THAT BOOKS

"How many lumps would you like in your coffee, Mr Perkins ?"

Martha's call to pick her husband up from the office party was unexpectedly early.

The lavatory suction was unusually high that day.

Unfortunately the 'Emergency Exit' sign had been put in the wrong place.

Perkins was pleasantly surprised when the staff paid for his first cruise.

Directions to a new customer.

Suddenly Perkins experienced 5G as the rockets attached to his seat ignited.

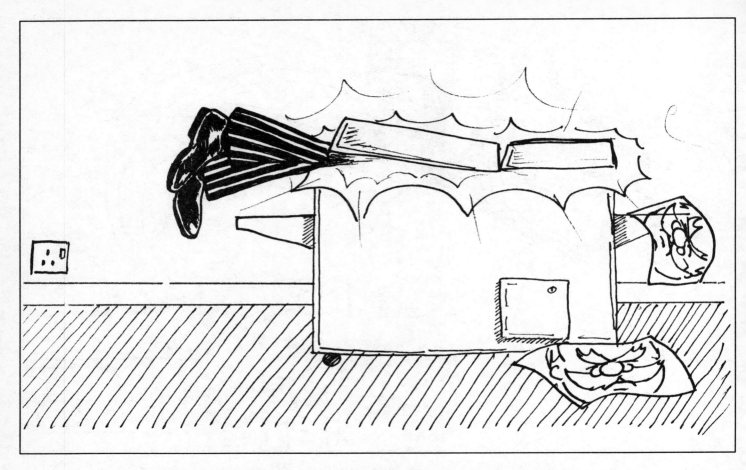

The photocopier had been a problem since the day it arrived.

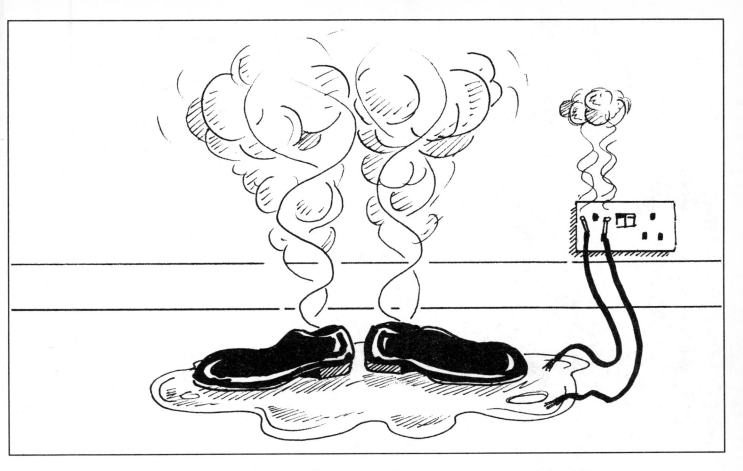

It took more than 50,000 Watts to make Perkins 'spontaneously' combust.

Perkins was suspicious about the amount of string being ordered.

It was news to Perkins that public toilets closed early for the Bank Holiday.

Perkins was just about to point out they were on the wrong side of the motorway, when the taxi driver jumped out.

The fax machine seemed to reach out and grab Perkins' tie.

Sales were bad.

The hotel staff hadn't told Perkins about the drought.

The new director's chair wasn't what Perkins had expected.

Terry's breathing seemed a little strained.

The new cash machine didn't just retain his card.

The outward-bound course seemed a little arduous.

Like a shopping trolley, the fork-lift truck sometimes acted as if it had a mind of its own.

The local police couldn't believe their luck when they were tipped-off about the serial killer in their village.

Perkins didn't realise swallowing a fly was so serious.

Perkins made a mental note never to criticise Tracy's choice of sandwich filling again.

How a frisbee could reach the 43rd floor was beyond Perkins.

The old exploding-cigar routine.

Terry's bruised finger meant he couldn't carry the days takings to the bank.

The sturdy oak table had been there since Perkins' great-great-grandfather founded the company.

Unsafe electrical wiring.

It was the last time he would ask Tracy to book economy seats.

Perkins didn't realise Terry's eyesight was so bad.

**Perkins couldn't understand why nobody else thought Tracy's idea
of hand-feeding the lions was a good one.**

The automatic cut-out on the lawn mower signalled its dissent in a flash of green sparks.

Hard sell.

Perkin's 'Good Management' books were tired of being ignored.

The telephone receiver seemed to rise up like a charmed snake and wrap itself around a startled Perkins.

Doctor Smith agreed - he had never heard of anyone catching a deadly virus from a computer before.

Killer paperclips.

Tracy's lessons in Spanish had let Perkins down.

The personnel department had a fantastic new overseas posting for Perkins.

Perkins thought the courier would only take his package.

Perkins thought his tip was more than enough.

Water pistols had come a long way since Perkins was a child.

Loose strings on a Newton's cradle.

Perkins would never try to cut back on hotel expenses again.

Having settled many office disputes, Perkins thought the latest argument a little contrived.

The workmen usually secured their equipment before going home.

How to turn back was the second lesson.

The advertising agency said Perkins should appear somewhere in the commercial.

Traditional shaving methods give a closer cut.

The second drawer seemed to slide open while the top drawer was in use.

Computer error could not be blamed for the extra zeros and the word 'overdrawn'.

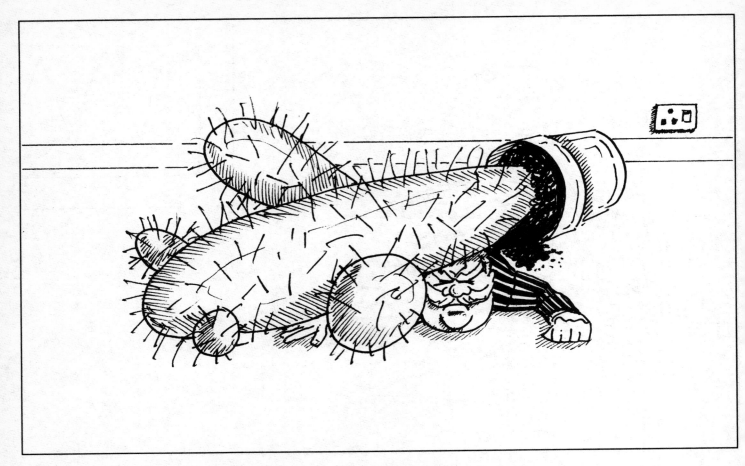

Nobody knew who the office cactus belonged to.

The marketing manager said it was a good idea.

The pet shop owner's assurances were misplaced.

A gentlemanly game of golf.

Tracy's children rarely visited the office, Perkins didn't like kids.

Annual staff versus management cricket match.

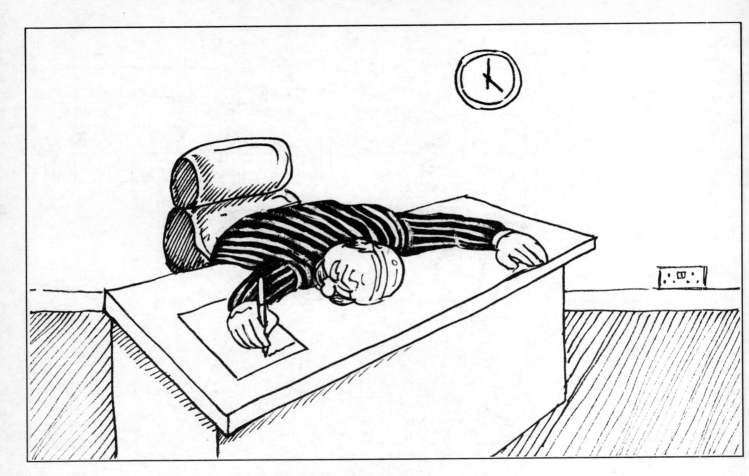

Poison pen letters.

On reflection, a multi-story car park wasn't a good place to push start a car.

The screen said ''Hit any key'', but before Perkins could move the keyboard struck first.

Tracy usually did the stapling.

132 different gears but no brakes.

Terry's research had located the exact piece of ground beneath the hole in the ozone layer.

Bungee elastics have a weight limit.

Tracy's holiday in Switzerland had been a great success.

Sometimes Tracy's ideas for charity fund-raising seemed a little bizarre.

Under the affluence of incahol, Perkins thought he could fly - hic.

The new contract office cleaners single-mindedly set about their job.

Terry had picked an odd time to ask for help repairing the lightening conductor.

The springs in Perkins' briefcase seemed to be getting stronger.

His new glasses were just the job.

Perkins had heard that Heli-Skiing was exciting.

Perkins liked books, but he would never have placed his copy of
'Advanced Engineering Techniques' on the top shelf - he knew it wasn't strong enough.

ACME Ltd didn't usually employ an Australian International prop forward.

"Four what ?"

Perkins didn't know how his arm went up when the knife-thrower asked for volunteers.

There seemed to be a problem with the zip on his new trousers.

**The new light-weight miniature electronically-controlled parachute
proved inadequate for the charity jump.**

Perkins remembered thinking his new desk-clock had an unusually loud tick.

A mysterious hand appeared and filled his glass without Perkins noticing.

Terry's method of stacking his load had never let him down before.

"Hold these" said the car repair man.

The dolphin seemed to have grown.

One bauble too many.

After hearing "Ready", the instructor never looked back.

Helping at the clay-pigeon shoot was not Perkins' idea of fun.

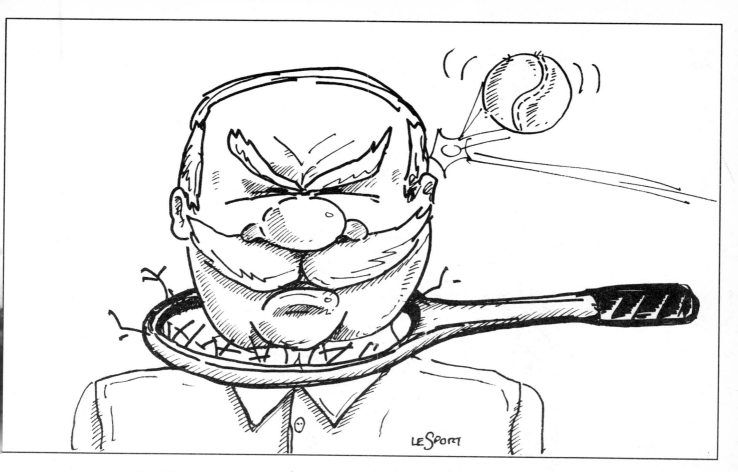

Perkins was astounded how easily he beat the club president with the new racquet given to him by the staff.

Radio-controlled champagne corks.

It was the last time Perkins was going out at night dressed casually.

The case of the missing pen had got totally out of hand.

Nearly an hour later the fly eventually landed.

Just relax.

Perkins had never selected 'Exercise Level 3' before.

Tracy's pen-friends seemed very friendly.